GW01454214

The Last Prince of Wales 1983
has been published as a
Limited Edition of which
this is

Number 26 l

A complete list of the original
subscribers is printed
at the back of the book

# THE LAST PRINCE OF WALES

Llywelyn ap Gruffydd, the last Prince of Wales.
(A reconstruction by Leslie Brooke from a surviving stone remnant of the 13th century found on the site of the Royal court at Aberffraw).

# THE LAST PRINCE OF WALES

Llywelyn and King Edward:
the end of the Welsh dream
1282-3

by

## DAVID STEPHENSON MA(Oxon)DPhil

BARRACUDA BOOKS LIMITED
BUCKINGHAM, ENGLAND
MCMLXXXIII

Published by Barracuda Books Limited
Buckingham, England
and Printed and Bound by
Nene Litho & Woolnough Bookbinding
Wellingborough, England

Jacket Printed by
Cheney & Sons Limited
Banbury, Oxon

Lithography by
Bicester Photolitho Limited
Bicester, England

Display set in Souvenir
and Text set in 12/14 Souvenir Light by
Bedfordshire Graphics Limited
Bedford, England

# Contents

All rights reserved. No part of this publication may be reproduced,
stored in a retrieval system, or transmitted, in any form or by any
means, electronic, mechanical, photocopying, recording or otherwise,
without the prior permission of Barracuda Books Limited.

Any copy of this book issued by the Publisher as clothbound or as a
paperback is sold subject to the condition that it shall not by way of
trade or otherwise, be lent, re-sold, hire out or otherwise circulated
without the Publisher's prior consent, in any form of binding or cover
other than that in which it is published, and without a similar condition
including this condition being imposed on a subsequent purchaser.

# Foreword

*by Emeritus Professor Sir Idris Ll. Foster*

The seventh centenary of the death of Llywelyn ap Gruffydd in December 1282 has been an occasion for recalling and reassessing the career and character of the man who in 1267 was formally recognised by the English King as the first 'Prince of Wales' and died, in mysterious circumstances, as the last Welsh Prince of Wales, near the river Irfon close to Builth towards dusk on that eleventh day of December.

In the final chapter of the *History of Wales* Sir John Lloyd describes 'the last stage . . . in the history of Wales under native rule'. 'At no period,' he writes, 'is the interest of the story more personal; for from beginning to end the tale of these twenty-six years centres in the doings of Llywelyn ap Gruffydd, who is not only the foremost of the princes of Wales, but also the single force which is of any account in Welsh politics'. For Sir John, the war of 1277 was the beginning of what he calls 'the downfall', and in the last majestic paragraph of his great work he says that 'it was for a distant generation to see that the last Prince had not lived in vain, but by his life-work had helped to build solidly the enduring fabric of Welsh nationality'.

One of the most distinguished of that 'distant generation', Sir Goronwy Edwards, has — especially in the introduction to his exemplary edition of *Littere Wallie* (1940) — examined, with his customary control of detail

9

and acute understanding, the constitutional significance of Llywelyn's 'principality' in its relationship both to Wales and to England. Llywelyn was the builder and maker of the principality of Wales. As Sir Goronwy remarked, 'a career so long, so eventful, and in some ways so puzzling has many sides.' Llywelyn's 'diagnosis' of the need of Wales was 'perfectly correct': 'some substantial measure of consolidation whereby it might be subjected "to the judgement of one king and to a single lordship".' To achieve this, Llywelyn required not only that vigorous purposefulness which he so clearly demonstrated in his activities but also an adequate redeeming of time to establish his suzerainty.

Among a yet younger generation of scholars who throughout the past twenty years have brought further knowledge and fresh interpretations of the 'age' and puzzles of Llywelyn ap Gruffydd Dr David Stephenson has earned for himself a place in the front row. After distinguishing himself in the Final Honour School of Modern History at Oxford, he undertook postgraduate work in examining the 'governance' of Wales in the twelfth and thirteenth centuries. In addition to applying the fundamental disciplines which he had been taught as an undergraduate, he acquired further competence in the languages of his essential sources, not least a sensitive knowledge of mediaeval Welsh. He became increasingly familiar both with the political and constitutional issues in his field of enquiry and with the character of each of the *dramatis personae* who had a part on the stage of this theatre.

It is on the basis of his close study of the complex web of men and circumstances that he has now written this short book on the events of the conflict of 1282-3. At one level it is skilful straightforward narrative; at the same time it

10

probes the responses and motives of the people, Welsh, English and others, who were involved in the developing nexus of events which led — to use Sir John Lloyd's phrase — to 'the turning point... in the contest between Welsh independence and the English crown'. In his interpretation, for example, of what happened at 'Irfon Bridge', he has aimed at a judicious summing-up of differing accounts in various chronicles. His analysis of Llywelyn's responsibility, judgement and strategy differs in emphasis from that of other historians. He draws proper attention to the lesser force of the energy and ambitions of Llywelyn's younger brother, the *infelix et infortunatus* Dafydd. Throughout his narrative Dr Stephenson has, I believe, succeeded in bringing together the criss-cross strands of diplomacy, tactics and military logistics to form a lucid and delicately controlled account of those fateful eighteen months.

To one who had the privilege of assisting David Stephenson on the first steps of the pathway which has led him to the high road of mediaeval Welsh history it is a gratifying pleasure to be allowed to offer this foreword in commendation.

11th December 1982

# Preface

This book is a product of some twelve years of research into thirteenth-century Welsh history. That research began as an enquiry into the methods of government of the thirteenth-century princes. But in the course of the work, I became convinced that there was, in the final tragic months of Llywelyn ap Gruffydd and his brother Dafydd, a story of immense power, if only it could be unravelled from evidence which is often obscure and ambiguous. I have tried to tell that story here, and to convey at a distance of seven hundred years, something of the atmosphere of those months.

In the shaping of the book I have amassed more debts of gratitude than I can express here. I should like however to thank Emeritus Professor Sir Idris Foster, both for agreeing to write the Foreword, and for years of advice and encouragement; my publisher Clive Birch for the skill and patience with which he has guided the production of the book, and for the more than ordinary faith which he has placed in it and its author; my colleague Bruce Lorimer for drawing the maps, artist Leslie Brooke for his masterly interpretation of the Prince's head from a photographed stone remnant and for his heraldic beasts, and my wife, Charlotte, for her enthusiasm and support, and her invaluable services as typist and critic.

# The Poetry of Welsh Names

Non-Welsh readers will gain a lot if they can capture something of the poetry which lies within the Welsh language and which is expressed even in the names of people and places. Here, therefore, are a few guidelines on pronunciations, which will help to bring Welsh names to life, and will hint at their beauty.

Welsh *dd* is similar to English *th* in *th*is
Welsh *f* is similar to English *v*
Welsh *ff* is similar to English *f*
Welsh *ll* has no equivalent in English. Place the tip of the tongue on the roof of the mouth and expel breath with a hiss. Alternatively, pronounce as *thl*
Welsh *u* is similar to English *u,* in bu*s*y
Welsh *w* is similar to English *oo*
Welsh *y* has a sharp sound, like English *i,* when it is the final syllable of a word, and a dull sound, like English *uh* when it stands on its own or before the final syllable of a word
Welsh *oe* is similar to English *oi* in *oi*l
Welsh *ch* is similar to Scots *ch* in *lo*ch
The stress in a Welsh word normally falls on the final syllable but one
The word *ap* or *ab* in a Welsh name denotes 'son of '
Some examples:
Gruffydd = Grifith
Maredudd = Meredith
Hywel = Howel
Fychan = Vuchan
Cwm Hir = Coom Heer

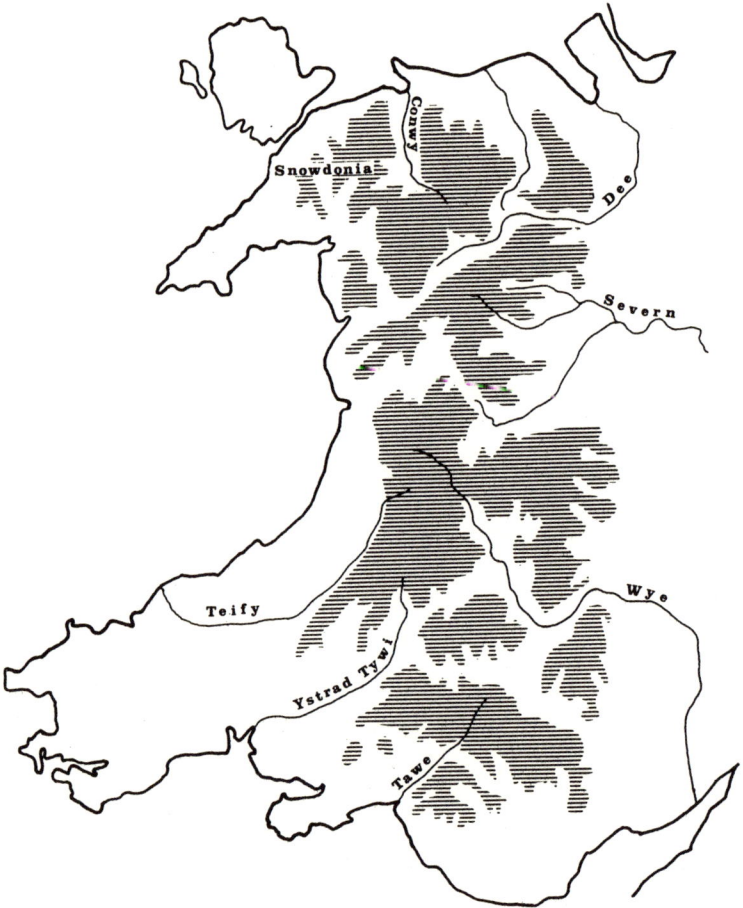

Land over 800 feet

Physical map of Wales.

14

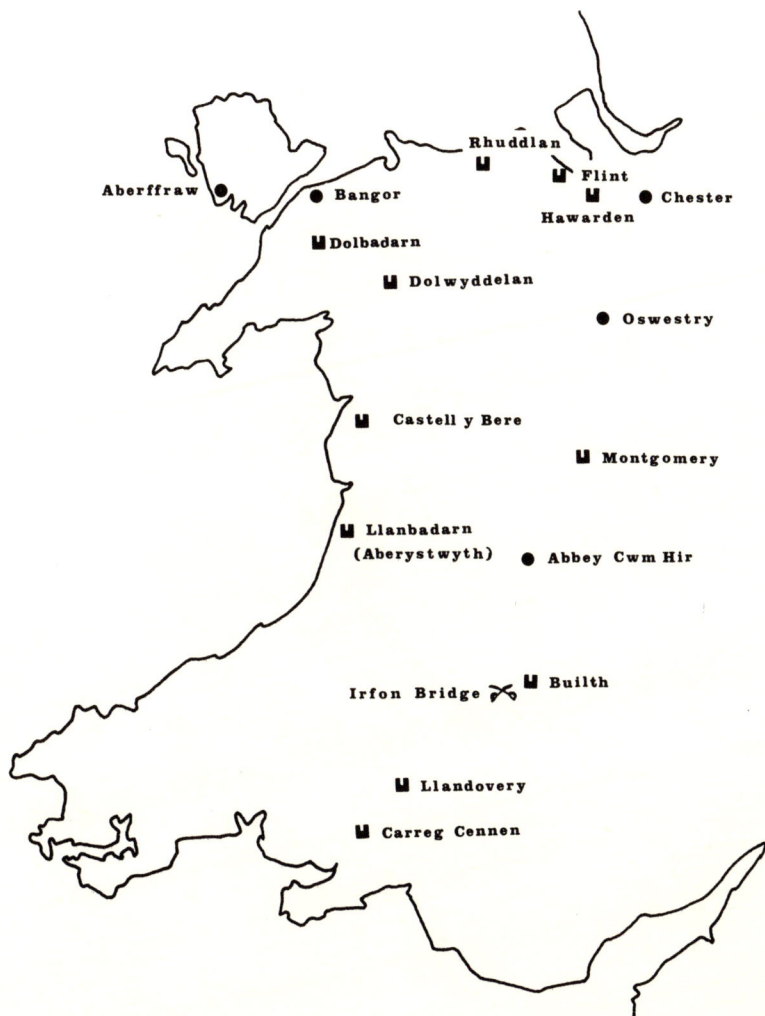

■ Principal Castles in 1282

Rhuddlan
Flint
Aberffraw    Bangor    Hawarden    Chester
Dolbadarn
Dolwyddelan
Oswestry
Castell y Bere
Montgomery
Llanbadarn
(Aberystwyth)    Abbey Cwm Hir
Irfon Bridge ✕    Builth
Llandovery
Carreg Cennen

Principal places in 1282 Wales.

15

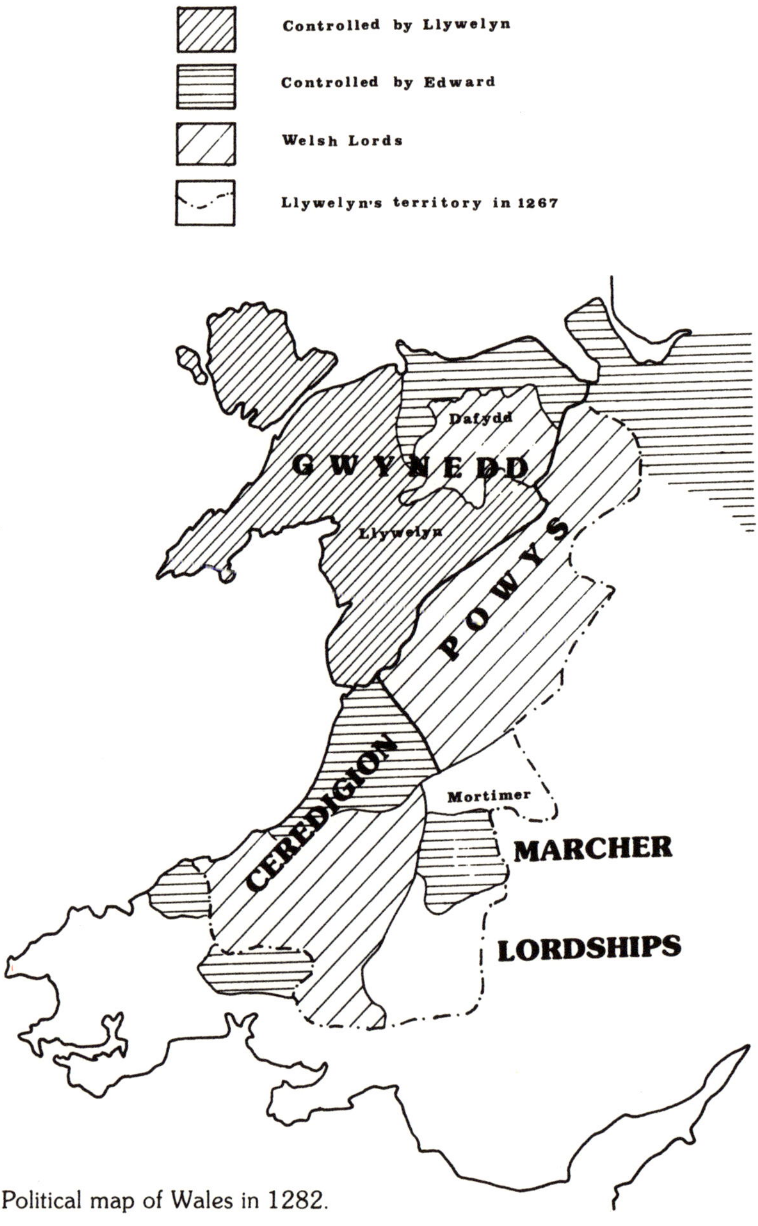
Controlled by Llywelyn
Controlled by Edward
Welsh Lords
Llywelyn's territory in 1267
Dafydd
GWYNEDD
Llywelyn
POWYS
CEREDIGION
Mortimer
MARCHER
LORDSHIPS

Political map of Wales in 1282.

 I

# Aftermath

For the five thousand Welshmen fighting Edward I's war in Flanders, the winter of 1297 was no easy time: they were ill-clothed, ill-paid, and ill-equipped. When the northerners among them had been recruited, it had proved impossible at first to select troop-leaders, for the King's officials reported that there was not one in the land who had an adequate mount. And when they had been shipped to Flanders, the chronicler Lodewyk van Velthem marvelled that 'in the very depth of winter they were running about bare legged . . . Their weapons were bows, arrows and swords. They also had javelins. They wore linen clothes, and were great drinkers. They did a lot of damage to the Flemings, for their pay was too little, and so they took what did not belong to them'.

Among that ragged army served Rhys Fychan, Cynan ap Maredudd and his brother Gruffydd ap Maredudd. Time was when they had been lords of the land of Ceredigion, each with his court, his entourage of guards and servants, his steward, his falconer, his huntsmen, but that was long ago, before the calamity. Wales had new masters now, and the old lords, they had nothing 'save of God and the king'. The revolts had failed, their leaders made captive or executed, and Edward had covered the country with his garrisons, his towns full of English settlers, his castles, raised up by his Savoyard builders, at Conwy,

Caernarfon, Harlech, Beaumaris, Flint, Rhuddlan, Aberystwyth, Builth.

And so Rhys, Cynan and Gruffydd fought for the alien King's meagre wage: even that was better than lying fettered in his prisons, as had been their lot for years. Some of their erstwhile comrades in arms had fared worse: Rhys Wyndod, lord of part of the Vale of Tywi was held at Windsor, existing on 4½d per day. His brother Llywelyn ap Rhys of Is Cennen had also been a captive for nearly fifteen years by 1297, and was destined to remain such for many years more, his robes becoming threadbare, his bedding rotten. He was lodged in the Tower of London. In that same year, the men who haunted the taverns close by the Tower would point out to strangers an object impaled on an iron spike, high over the royal fortress: it was the skull of Llywelyn ap Gruffydd.

# II

# Gathering of Lords

It had been agreed that Dafydd, the younger brother, should stay and guard the fastness of Snowdonia; Prince Llywelyn was to take men to raise the south against the incoming English forces.

That autumn of 1282, the two brothers were forced to trust each other, yet it must have struck their men as strange that Llywelyn and Dafydd were at last working in concert. Hostility and suspicion had long separated them. Thirty years earlier, possession of the principality of north Wales had been shared by three brothers, Llywelyn, Dafydd, and Owain, the sons of Gruffydd, son of Llywelyn the Great. The arrangement had not been satisfactory: quarrels had broken out between them, and in 1255 Owain and Dafydd had launched an attack on Llywelyn, intending to drive him from the land. The armies met at Bryn Derwin, where the gentle hills of the Llyn peninsula begin to rise towards the harsher peaks of Arfon and Eifionydd, the land of Snowdonia. The struggle that followed was seen by the poet Llygad Gwr, who, rapt with admiration for Llywelyn, sang of his prowess in the fight:

He lamented not the day when he assaulted his foes,
A hero descended from the brave.
I saw him struggle with hosts of men,
An honourable man, shunning disgrace.

He that saw Llywelyn, fiery dragon,
In the conflict of Arfon and Eifionydd,
Saw how hard it was
To stem his fury in the mountain pass.

Llywelyn's victory at Bryn Derwin gave him possession of the whole of north Wales, and of his brothers, whom he cast into prison. For him it was the beginning of a rise to a renown not hitherto attained by any Welsh ruler. Over the next dozen years Llywelyn had cleared English armies from his borders, and crushed rivals for power, until he held all the ancient northern realm of Gwynedd, from the river Dyfi in the south-west to the Dee estuary in the east. There soon followed the assertion of his supremacy over the petty Welsh chiefs of Powys, in mid-Wales, and Deheubarth in the south. Llygad Gwr was ecstatic in his praise of the lion of Cemais, the dragon of Arfon, the war-wolf of Eryri, eagle of Snowdon, brave lion of Mon; Llywelyn was the ruler of four languages, the governor of the three provinces of Wales, the true King of that land.

And in 1267 he had compelled Henry III of England to accept his greatness: Llywelyn was recognised as Prince of Wales — the only Welsh ruler ever to be so acknowledged by the English. Llywelyn's principal court at Aberffraw in Anglesey became the centre of the new realm of Wales for which the poets had clamoured. The Welsh lawyers had long proclaimed the superior dignity of the lord who ruled from Aberffraw: he was the Mechdeyrn, the overlord. Now the vision was a reality. At Llywelyn's court were gathered not only his servants from the north, but the lords of Powys and Deheubarth. They knelt before him and placed their hands between his in the act of homage; they received their lands from him; they swore fealty to him; they settled their disputes by his judgements; and when they erred they languished in his prisons.

They came to his courts with mixed expectations of wonder and fear. The castles of Snowdonia inspired respect and nervousness, but Aberffraw, set on the edge of the western sea, was the chief court, impressive and not a little mysterious; adorned with the carved stone heads of Llywelyn's forebears, the Princes of Gwynedd. A fabled place, known to the storytellers as the legendary court at which Bran the Blessed, lord of the island of Britain, had entertained Matholwch, King of Ireland, and bestowed upon him Branwen Daughter of Llyr. And Bran had been a hero of magical powers; his severed head had been carried for years, uncorrupted, by his companions, bringing joy to their feasts, until they buried it at London, in the White Mount. But none of the rulers of the past, whose sculpted eyes stared out at the feasting in that hall, nor any of the fabulous heroes with whom legend populated the court, could compare with the vanquisher of England, the crowned one of Aberffraw, Llywelyn, son of Gruffydd, Prince of Wales, lord of Snowdon.

For his brothers, defeat at Bryn Derwin was the opening of very different stories. Owain was to spend over two decades, almost all of his remaining life, incarcerated in Dolbadarn castle, while the more forthright of the bards lamented the long imprisonment of 'the man in the tower'. Dafydd was more fortunate; quickly released and employed by Llywelyn to lead his armies, his services to the Prince were rewarded with the grant of wide and rich territories. But he was still the dependent of Llywelyn, and his affections still lay with Owain, whom he burned to liberate.

Twice, therefore, in the following years, Dafydd had left Llywelyn's side and fled to the English, ever prepared to welcome deserters from the upstart Prince. The aftermath of the second desertion was still a vivid memory in 1282,

22

for Dafydd had played a central role in the events which had brought his brother close to ruin.

In 1274 Dafydd had plotted with the lord of Southern Powys, Gruffydd ap Gwenwynwyn, to assassinate the Prince. On a given night in February, Gruffydd's son was to bring a band of armed men in secret to the court; they would be admitted by Dafydd, and would then kill Llywelyn. Dafydd would be proclaimed prince, and Gruffydd's family would be rewarded with territories. But the carrying out of the plot was delayed by bad weather, so that the assassins were unable to reach the court, and then details of the conspiracy were betrayed to the Prince. In panic, Dafydd and Gruffydd fled for protection to England, where they were well received by the King, Edward I. They spent the next few years launching raids into Wales, plundering and burning in Llywelyn's lands. And in 1277 Dafydd had helped King Edward's soldiery to launch a crushing attack on the Prince, which left Llywelyn bereft of all but north-west Wales, the heartland of Gwynedd.

From Llywelyn's downfall Dafydd had reaped great profit: English estates, an English wife of noble family, Elizabeth Ferrars, and much land in north-east Wales had been conferred upon him by a grateful King.

Yet here were Dafydd and Llywelyn, five years on, brothers in arms.

Each had come to feel bitterness at the new dispensation in Wales ushered in by the war of 1277. Dafydd felt that his services to Edward had not been adequately rewarded: the King had at first promised him a larger share of north Wales than he had, in the event, received. And he was resentful of the harassment of his lands and men by the Royal officials whom Edward had introduced to govern the conquered territories. To many of them it mattered little that Dafydd had been the King's ally: he was a Welshman, and so fair game for oppression. The transfer of his loyalties had by now become an easy thing for him, and the opening months of 1282 saw him preparing to fulfill his ambitions by rebellion against his King and erstwhile protector.

On the night of 21/22 March, Dafydd struck. His men overwhelmed the castle of Hawarden, near the Cheshire border, killing the garrison and capturing its lord, Roger de Clifford. Within days, rebellion flared throughout north and west Wales. On 22 March, a large force of Welsh nobles and their followers attacked the Shropshire border town of Oswestry and carried off the goods of the townsfolk as plunder. Two days later Gruffydd ap Maredudd, one of the lords of Ceredigion, appeared at Aberystwyth, where the Constable of the Royal castle was about to hold the local courts in the King's name. Gruffydd apparently came in peace; he invited the Constable to dine with him. It was a trick, to lure the official from the castle: when he came out, he was seized, and Gruffydd's men ran through the town, killing the English settlers, and then took over the castle itself. On 26 March more of the southern lords captured the castles of Llandovery and Carreg Cennen, and on the following day, Good Friday, it was once more the turn of Oswestry to suffer: a still larger Welsh force returned to the town and burned it.

Everywhere in the west and the north-east the King's men were being killed or driven out.

But what of Prince Llywelyn? His part in these events is so shadowy that we may easily believe that he merely followed the lead given by his turbulent younger brother. But that would be to mistake the man. True, Llywelyn had appeared to accept Edward I's supremacy in the years after the war of 1277, but he had not been cowed or reduced to a servile obedience: the diplomatic atmosphere between the two had frequently been strained. He was incited to defiance by his own followers, who felt keenly the humiliations imposed upon them. Thus at Christmas, 1277, Llywelyn and the handful of Welsh lords still under his rule had gone with their retinues to London, to perform homage to the King. Their men were quartered in Islington and surrounding villages, where the local people deeply offended them by congregating to laugh at their outlandish appearance and manners. The story runs that, so outraged were the Welsh, they secretly agreed to rebel at the first opportunity, resolving to die in their native land rather than come again to London as subjects to be held in derision.

Edward had indeed humbled the Prince in 1277 but, in his long career, Llywelyn had suffered other reverses, and yet had risen to greatness. It could happen again. And so, while he appeared to treat the King with all due deference, he laboured to regain his lost power.

Within his own territories the Prince persecuted those who had been disloyal to him in the last war. As early as 1278, one of the leading men of Anglesey, Iorwerth Foel, was complaining in Edward's Parliament that because of his past loyalty to the Royal cause, Llywelyn had seized his horses and grain, burned his houses and driven him from his lands. Another Anglesey man, Iorwerth ap Gruffydd, was also reported to be kept from his lands in retribution for having taken the King's side, while similar treatment was meted out to another Royal partisan, Madog ab Einion, a nobleman who held lands in the Llŷn peninsula. A former official of the Prince, Rhys ap Gruffydd ab Ednyfed, who had turned against Llywelyn during the war, was fined by his former master for showing contempt to him when on a visit to the court at Aberffraw in 1280;

the fine was a massive one, £100 — as much as the Prince raised in taxes from the whole of Anglesey in a year. Nor were ecclesiastics immune; the Bishop of Bangor, who in 1277 had fled to the King with tales of Llywelyn's oppressive behaviour, was subjected to the Prince's anger over the next few years, in spite of appeals from the King and the Archbishop of Canterbury for a reconciliation.

That Llywelyn should give vent to his wrath against those of his subjects who had opposed or deserted him was to be expected, however, and of itself signified little. Far more sinister were the Prince's efforts to bring the nobles of Wales, who had become the King's men in 1277, back under his own lordship.

Within a year of his defeat, Llywelyn had persuaded the chief minister of his old enemy, the lord of Southern Powys, to return to unity with him, and to try to induce his master to do likewise. That indeed would be an uphill task, for since the assassination plot of 1274 the rift between Llywelyn and Gruffydd ap Gwenwynwyn went deep. And now a complex legal struggle for the possession of extensive lands in mid-Wales was pending between them. Yet the Prince had clearly not yet given up hope of winning his former vassal back to his side.

Further south, the prospects for Llywelyn were better. The southern lords had tended to support King Edward in the war of 1277, but many were now regretting that decision. Llywelyn's rule had been high-handed at times, but now the interference and oppression of Royal bailiffs seemed to many the more grievous. And they heard some strange reports of Edward I. In the course of a legal case in 1279, one of the King's Welsh allies had blurted out a protest against an attempt to make him plead by Welsh law: such law did not apply, he cried, for the King proposed to supress it. It was the sort of statement which sent tremors of alarm through the ranks of the Welsh magnates.

Llywelyn's courts, especially the castle of Dolwyddelan, now became the scene of gatherings of southern lords, who were living in exile or were fast being alienated by the multitude of Royal officials applying a plethora of Royal regulations in and around their territories. Gruffydd and Cynan ap Maredudd, and Rhys ap Rhys ap Maelgwn, of Ceredigion, Hywel ap Rhys Gryg of Ystrad Tywi and Llywelyn ap Rhys Fychan of Is Cennen were all visitors to Dolwyddelan in the years after 1277.

Typical of the malcontents was Gruffydd ap Maredudd. While Iorwerth Foel of Anglesey was complaining in the 1278 Parliament about Llywelyn's tyranny, Gruffydd ap Maredudd was petitioning the same body for better treatment from the King. He had, he claimed, laboured greatly in the King's cause during the war, and yet had been deprived of half of his lands, so that he could scarcely maintain himself. All that he got in reply was a vague promise to look into the case. In such resentments Llywelyn found fertile ground in which to sow seeds of disaffection against the Royal domination of Wales.

And so Gruffydd ap Maredudd and his fellow lords began once more to accept Llywelyn's leadership, and even to help in bringing leading men of the south back under his lordship.

In yet other areas, scores of petty irritations combined to turn many a Welsh baron into a potential rebel against the King. One such was Llywelyn Fychan ap Gruffydd, one of the lords of Northern Powys, a man known to the poets as the dragon of Chirk. In the war of 1277 he had been quick to make his peace with the King, and had been rewarded with the promise that he would never again be placed under the lordship of the Prince. But Llywelyn Fychan's satisfaction with the new order was short-lived. Many of his countrymen resented his desertion of the Prince: after the sons of John fitzAlan, lord of Oswestry, had raided his lands, Llywelyn Fychan reported wistfully to the King that the Welsh, from whom he withdrew during the war, did not grieve much, but rejoiced at his vexation and damage. And gradually the catalogue of wrongs done to him by the King's men mounted: the Royal Constable of Oswestry had deprived him of lands and pastures; both he and his men had been unjustly imprisoned; his men had been assaulted when trying to sell goods in English markets; Royal officials had allowed him to be unjustly drawn into costly litigation — it had cost him £200 to defend one case alone.

Well might the Prince nurture the hope that in time the streams of resentment against the tyranny of Royal officials might grow into a great flood, which would wash down from the hills and clear the detritus of alien rule from Wales. In 1282, Llywelyn Fychan was to be among those who rose against Edward I.

Some lords held back from the rising, for they were sure of their ability to prosper under Royal rule. The most substantial of them were Gruffydd ap Gwenwynwyn of Southern Powys, who had rejected Llywelyn's attempts at reconciliation, and Rhys ap Maredudd, lord of Ystrad Tywi and the greatest of the southern magnates. But such absentees were few; unity prevailed, as never before, among the proud and susceptible Welsh barons, and behind it there surely lay the assiduous working of Llywelyn, five years of plotting and persuasion.

Someone had planned the rising: the outbreaks, though widely scattered, were almost simultaneous. Dafydd, some ten years Llywelyn's junior, was best fitted to provide military leadership, but authority rested with the Prince. One of Llywelyn's own officials was among those who attacked Oswestry on 22 March, and in the attacks on the Royal castles in the south and west were to be found the southern magnates with whom Llywelyn had been forging close links since 1277. Within days the Prince himself was helping to besiege the Royal castles of Flint and Rhuddlan. Soon the list of Llywelyn's adherents reads like one of the recitations of the names of heroes in mediaeval Welsh romances. There came to his side Gruffydd Fychan, lord of Ial, he who was the ancestor of Owain Glyn Dwr; Llywelyn Fychan, his brother, the dragon of Chirk, lord of Nanheudwy and Cynllaith; Gruffydd and Elise, sons of Iorwerth, and Dafydd ap Gruffydd ab Owain, the lords of Edeirnion; Llywelyn Fychan's sons from Mechain, proud but impoverished survivors of an ancient ruling house. There came Rhys Fychan ap Rhys ap Maelgwn, who had been driven in 1277 from his lands south of the Dyfi, to take refuge with the Prince in Meirionydd. The south also gave to the rebellion Rhys Wyndod, Gruffydd, Hywel and Llywelyn, the sons of Rhys Ieuanc of Ystrad Tywi, Hywel ap Rhys Gryg of the same land, and Gruffydd and Cynan ap Maredudd, lords of Ceredigion. From the far south came Morgan ap Maredudd: not for the last time did he stand as a rebel against King Edward; not for the last time did he mysteriously survive.

These men were of ancient princely descent, of the stock of kings. For once every petty Welsh chief had called himself a king. With them joined others of lesser pedigree, though still noble, as Goronwy ap Heilyn of Gwynedd, whose family had served the northern princes for four generations and who was himself the steward of Dafydd ap Gruffydd: there was Madog ab Arawdr of Mallaen in the south, who had helped in the taking of

Llandovery and Carreg Cennen, and Dafydd ab Einion of Anglesey, steward of Prince Llywelyn and scion of a bardic stock, whose ancestors had praised the rulers of Gwynedd over a century ago. They made up a fine company, for here were representatives of every major ruling house in Wales, and of the wisest counsellors of the lords and princes. By the splendour of their lineage alone they called powerfully to Welshmen of every degree to join the onslaught on the English. They had at their back the formidable natural fortress of Snowdonia and Meirionydd, studded with the Prince's castles, and behind them also the great granary of Anglesey, so fertile that it had long been known as Mon, the mother of Wales. Her sons were to need sustenance, for after the first swift victories the odds against them were terrible.

# III

# *The King's Wrath*

Within four days of the fall of Hawarden, Edward I took steps to deal with the Welsh rising. From the outset it was clear that this formidable monarch was organising a crushing retaliation. Commanders were appointed — at first the Royal officials on the spot, but these were soon reinforced or superseded by noblemen of the first rank. The Earl of Gloucester was to command in the south-west, aided by Robert Tibetot, the Justiciar of West Wales and one of Edward's most trusted officials; the Earl of Hereford, Constable of England, took command in the area around Brecon; Roger Mortimer, one of the great magnates of the borderland, was placed in charge at Montgomery, aided by the Earl of Lincoln, and Reginald de Grey, Justiciar of Chester, was put at the head of the forces being assembled to strike into north Wales. By 8 April the King was ready to set off himself, 'to repress the rebellion and malice of the Welsh' as he put it. On the same day Edward wrote to Margaret, Queen of France, to inform her that the help which he had promised her for a war which she was waging in Provence would no longer be forthcoming: he needed all of his resources to put down the rebellion in Wales.

The Royal armies were going to strike at the rebels from several directions at once. And the attack would not come by land alone: the Cinque Ports were ordered to prepare ships for a seaborne force, and by July a fleet of over fifty vessels had been assembled off the north Welsh coast, ready for an assault on Anglesey.

Soon half of Europe was involved. Italian bankers, principally the great merchant banking house of the Riccardi of Lucca, were approached for massive loans with which to finance the coming campaign; to France was sent the Earl of Warwick to procure extra horses. From La Ferte-Milon in Champagne, the King's brother, Edmund of Cornwall wrote in May that he was settling his affairs in that region as quickly as he could, and would then take ship for England, bringing with him, if the King wished it, a contingent of troops from Champagne. Orders to recruit cavalry and crossbowmen were sent out to Edward's continental domains, to Ponthieu and Gascony. Eventually they came, a host of swaggering Gascon nobles and their retinues, lured by lucrative contracts: the Count of Armagnac, the Count of Bigorre, the Lord of Bergerac, the Viscount of Tarcazin, and many more, as the year wore on, until the flower of the Gascon nobility was with Edward.

For some of his troops the King did not have to look so far afield. Old adversaries of Llywelyn among the Welsh lords would do him good service: Gruffydd ap Gwenwynwyn of Southern Powys in the eastern areas, and Rhys ap Maredudd of Ystrad Tywi in the south were to put their forces at his disposal. Of the troops recruited by Edward, the composition of the cavalry was particularly diverse: the greater men, barons and the like, rode the massive war horses, the dextrarii, worth 100 marks each; the knights generally rode animals worth little more than 30 marks, while the other cavalry (the men at arms), were frequently mounted on horses with a value of but 10 marks. For all of these mounts some form of defensive coat was usual, the larger and more powerful steeds being capable of supporting a covering of chain mail, while for the lesser horses, coats of boiled leather were more the rule.

The same distinction applied to the riders: the best equipped wore suits of mail, augmented by great protective helms and shields of metal, while the bulk of the horsemen substituted at least some leather for mail in their suits. The common weapons were longsword and lance. Of the infantry, the most formidable in the eyes of contemporaries were the crossbowmen. The crossbow, generally made of Spanish yew and whalebone, was a complex weapon; its operator had to stand on a stirrup attached to the stock, in order to gain enough purchase to haul the cord over the trigger. It was a weapon not often found in the hands of the English infantry levies: its proper use required training, and virtually presupposed that its operator would be a professional soldier. The majority of the crossbowmen on whom Edward could call were Gascons, who served to the number of 1,500; only about 250 English crossbowmen were present in his armies. The weapon which they wielded was, at short range, murderous: the heavy quarrel which it shot would kill or maim even a well-protected adversary.

The remainder of the infantry was called up from the counties near to the Welsh border, from the north Midland counties of Derbyshire and Nottinghamshire, and from the lordships of south Wales, Gwent, Glamorgan, Gower, Kidwelly, Llanstephan and Pembroke. Of these, most of the English were raw levies with little experience of, or appetite for warfare; the exceptions were the north Midlanders, the men of Sherwood Forest. Together with the south Welsh troops, these were expert archers. Their bows did not have the smashing power of the crossbow, but they were effective at long range and could be shot very rapidly. Here was the weapon which, in its developed form as the longbow, was to be the key to the dazzling English victories over the French in the 14th and early-15th centuries.

The bulk of the infantry available to Edward, that is the greater part of the English levies, was armed with spears, and, in some cases, with bows, though their meagre supplies of arrows suggest that the bow was not their primary weapon. Ill-equipped and inexperienced many of them might be, but still Edward strove to make them an effective force. He was careful not to call out too many infantry at once, and thus avoided unwieldy concentrations of troops: and he kept them in the field for three months at a time, longer than had been usual, so ensuring that they might develop some experience in warfare.

By the mid-summer, the numbers of troops assembled were daunting: hundreds of cavalry and crossbowmen, and thousands of foot-soldiers. Edward's entourage at Chester, where he made his first headquarters, included the Earls of Lancaster, Surrey, Norfolk and Warwick, each bringing his own retinue and troops. And to back up these massing armies, great stores of provisions and arms were assembled. 64,000 crossbow quarrels were ordered from Bristol and London; later another 70,000 were brought up for the Gascons. There arrived in addition hundreds of workmen to support the soldiers. In the north, Reginald de Grey was soon in charge of 730 woodmen, whose main task was to cut passes through the dense forest-lands, so as to lessen the danger of ambushes; then there were 340 carpenters and 40 masons, to repair fortifications slighted by the Welsh forces.

All manner of writs were now being issued to local officials throughout England, as the strength of the realm was gathered up to suppress the rising. No officials were more burdened than those in the counties adjacent to the March, the borderland of Wales. Typical was the stream of orders received by the Sheriff of Herefordshire, John de Burghull. In the course of the year following the attack on Hawarden, this harassed official was many times ordered to find fighting men for the King. On 20 May he was to issue a proclamation calling out all who held land of the King and owed him military service: they were to go with horses and arms to a rendezvous point at Rhuddlan. On 2 July that order was countermanded: the assembly point for the Herefordshire men was to be Montgomery, a sign perhaps of changed tactics, or an indication that the rebellion was becoming serious in mid-Wales. 24 November brought a command to assemble the strongest men-at-arms in the county so that the King's envoy, Hugh de Turberville, might choose a hundred of them for service; a further two hundred men were required on 6 December, and even on 21 March 1283 a further similar order required 400 footmen to be selected.

As well as fighting men, woodcutters and other auxiliaries were constantly required: earlier, on June 1, the Sheriff was told to choose 200 woodmen and charcoal-burners from among the strongest and most skilled men in the county, who were to be provided with wages and sent to Brecon, the Earl of Hereford's sector. Six weeks later another hundred wood-cutters were called for, with a further hundred demanded early in December. The burden of organising provisions and equipment for the soldiery and auxiliaries also fell upon the sheriffs. On 15 April John de Burghull was commanded to restrict markets in the county: provisions were to be sold only at

35

Whitchurch, or where Roger Mortimer was based. The whole activity of the shire was to be channelled towards the requirements of the King's forces in the area. Just over a month later came an order to issue a proclamation, that all with over £30 worth of land should have a strong horse, suitable for use in the war, which should be available for service. A writ of 8 November ordered the Sheriff to ensure that carters, or tranters, were not hindered while bringing provisions to the King, and urged him to see that twenty such carters should be constantly assigned to the task of taking goods to Chester. Again, the following year, on 21 March, the Sheriff was ordered to issue a proclamation that all those with victuals to sell should take them for sale to the King's army at Montgomery. Cash, too, was a constant Royal requirement, and the King's officials were expected to help in ensuring a ready supply: on 28 October de Burghull was commanded to send direct to the King the proceeds of a tax levied throughout the shire, and in February 1283 he was to send £20 to Chester without delay.

Edward had grasped that good organisation was necessary if the Welsh lords were to be defeated. The traditional Welsh method of dealing with an English attack was to lay waste the country of the lowlands, and to fall back, with their families and their beasts, into the mountains. It was a tactic which would work as long as the English were not efficient enough to bring up a ready supply of food, equipment and reinforcements. Then, ill-clothed, ill-supplied and hungry they would be subject to the harrying attacks of the Welsh in the hills around them, until they had no stomach for further fighting and a peace would be arranged.

A generation earlier, in the course of a Royal attack on Gwynedd, one English soldier had written of the plight of the army:

36

'We dwell here in watchings and fastings, in prayer, in cold and in nakedness. In watchings for fear of the Welsh, with their sudden raids on us by night. In fastings for lack of victuals, since the halfpenny loaf cannot be had for less than fivepence. In prayer that we may quickly return safely to our homes. In cold and nakedness for we live in houses of linen and have no winter clothes.'

But that had been in the days of Edward's father. The son was more formidable and more methodical. Little was now left to chance in the military build-up. The lessons of past errors had been learned. And the King would not tolerate slackness in his servants. The tone of many of the Royal mandates was threatening: the Mayor and citizens of Hereford were to hand over the proceeds of a tax to the Sheriff as quickly as possible, as they loved their bodies and their goods. The cash which the Sheriff himself was to send to Chester in 1283 was also to be despatched quickly, if he wished to avoid the King's everlasting wrath. An order to the Sheriff in March of 1283, to make ready a force of woodcutters, and to arrange for corn and victuals to be sent to the King, commanded that the official should come in person to Edward to certify that the order had been carried out, and threatened punishment on his person and all his goods if there should be any negligence.

Some local officials became decidedly panicky at the menacing tone of the orders being sent out to them. Thus, Henry du Lee, the Sheriff of Lancashire, wrote to Robert fitz John, the King's Marshal, to complain that he had received instructions to assemble 500 footmen at Chester — but had been given only a few days' notice. He was unable to comply, for his county was fifty leagues in length. What, he asked pitifully, was he to do? Should he come at once with as many men as he could collect, or come a few days later with the full complement?

Hard as he was on his own officials, Edward was yet prepared to be lenient in his treatment of the rebellious Welsh, if that lessened the scale of the task facing him. Early in the war he issued a proclamation to the rebels, assuring them that they would be allowed their liberty and their lands if they came rapidly to his peace, and served him faithfully. It was an offer which brought many defections from the Prince's side.

But however politic Edward showed himself in his readiness to forgive the insurgents, there was no concealing the intensity of his anger at the rebellion and those who had instigated it. Dafydd was singled out for special denunciation as a renegade:

'We welcomed him when an exile, endowed him out of our own lands, and favoured him under the cloak of our wing, placing him amongst the greatest of our palace.'

But if Dafydd had offended more grievously than any others, the Welsh as a race were frequently subjected to ringing denunciations, as in the preamble to the writs of summons to a parliament in 1283:

'The tongue of man can scarcely recount the variety of tricks and plots by which the Welsh, in the manner of wolves, have afflicted us and our predecessors from time out of memory; nor can it tell of the number of slaughters of magnates, English and others, of young and old men, of women and even of children; of the burning of castles and manors, both ours and those of our subjects, nor of the number of times they have disturbed our realm, fearing neither God nor man.'

By the time those writs were sent out, Edward and his soldiery had ensured that fear had touched the hearts of many in Wales.

# IV

# Games of War

The pattern of fighting in the war which began at the end of March 1282, resembles closely the manoeuvres which marked the ancient Welsh board game of gwyddbwyll. In that game a large number of attacking pieces would seek to entrap a king aided by a small number of defenders. The defenders' best hope of success lay in sudden darting sallies this way and that, in an attempt to disorganise the encircling attackers. For the latter, the principal danger of capture lay in over-eagerness to move in upon their quarry.

So it was in the months which followed the fall of Hawarden: Edward's accumulation of troops, in preparation for an advance from several directions at once, constantly threatened to drive back Llywelyn and Dafydd and their allies, and pen them in the rocky redoubts of Snowdonia and Meirionydd — such a strategy had worked before, in 1277, when the island granary of Anglesey had been captured and the Welsh worn down by a many-pronged attack. For such an assault to succeed it had to be carefully constructed and timed: the efforts of the regional commanders had to be concerted. It was thus not until the early summer that the Royal offensive began in earnest.

During June, Reginald de Grey in the north began to

push up the valley of the Dee, and by the end of the month he had taken Dafydd's castle of Hope. At the same time Edward, with the main northern force, worked along a line from Flint to Rhuddlan, which he made his base for the assembly of his fleet, and for the preparation of an attack on Dafydd's stronghold of Denbigh. In the northern sector, therefore, all was going according to Edward's plan: the lands to the east of the river Conwy were gradually being reconquered.

In the other main area of operations, however — the south-west — matters were otherwise. The local commander, the Earl of Gloucester, was preparing to recapture the castles taken by the rebels in the opening days of the conflict. In mid-June Carreg Cennen was occupied by a Royal force operating from the castle of Dinefwr. On 17 June the whole force moved back towards its base, laden with booty from the successful operation. At Llandeilo Fawr the returning men were intercepted by a body of Welsh troops, and heavily defeated. Among the dead was the son of William de Valence, Earl of Pembroke.

The defeat at Llandeilo Fawr was a signal warning against carelessness and over-confidence. For many weeks there were no more English advances in this area: clearly, more thorough preparations for its subjugation were needed. Among these was one ordered by Edward himself: Gloucester was relieved of his command, his place being taken, on 6 July, by the bereaved Earl of Pembroke. It was an ominous move: Valence's conduct of the war was unlikely to be anything less than determined.

In the eastern districts of central Wales there seems to have been no organised Welsh army to trouble the King's commanders, but unrest was widespread, so that all along the March large numbers of Edward's soldiery were kept in readiness.

Thus far, little had been heard of Llywelyn himself. For that there were good reasons. The Prince was now elderly, nearing 60 years of age, and he needed to conserve his strength. He had, moreover, good cause to remain in Gwynedd during the early summer. For his wife, Eleanor, was about to give birth to their first child. Llywelyn had waited long for an heir, as he had waited long for Eleanor. She was the daughter of Simon de Montfort, who had died a rebel against Henry III in the battle of Evesham in 1265. Some said that even before that date Llywelyn had asked for her hand; certainly he had arranged to marry Eleanor when she was living in exile in France in the early 1270s, and in 1275 she and a small group of companions had set sail for Wales, so that the wedding might take place. In the Channel, however, the bride's ship was intercepted by English vessels, which carried her off to Bristol, whence she was sent to the King. Edward had Eleanor imprisoned, and her incarceration became an element in the quarrels with Llywelyn which were to lead to the war of 1277. In the peace which followed that struggle, Edward's attitude to the marriage of Llywelyn and Eleanor softened, and the King even arranged for the two to be married in 1278 at Worcester Cathedral, meeting the expenses himself.

Now, four years later, the union promised to produce an heir for Llywelyn. He had taken a risk: by not marrying and producing children earlier, he had avoided the prospect of strife among sons for control of the Principality. By leaving marriage so late, however, he risked dying childless, in which case the land would be rent by a still greater number of rival claimants among his kin. Now, in June of 1282, came the birth of the long awaited child.

There was to be no male heir of Llywelyn's body: the baby was a girl, Gwenllian. And there was worse, for Eleanor died in giving birth. That month, therefore, two

41

groups departed from Gwynedd. One consisted of the small group of Eleanor's personal retainers: Richard le Tailleur, Hugh le Serjaunt, and Juliana Daunsele made their way under safe conduct into England, and thence, probably, into France. The second group was more purposeful: a body of armed men, led by the Prince himself, rode south.

It was an embittered man who turned from his personal tragedy to the conflict for his country. But he was still the war-wolf of Eryri: the blood of his enemies would wash away his sorrows. Thus Llywelyn burst across the Dyfi into Cyfeiliog and Ceredigion, and still further south into Ystrad Tywi, where the lands of Rhys ap Maredudd, Edward's ally, were burned and plundered. The Prince's arrival in the south sent a tremor through the southern March, especially in areas like Brecon, where the Earl of Hereford was struggling to contain rebellion among his own tenantry.

By August, however, with his fleet assembled off Rhuddlan, and with Pembroke having called up and organised reinforcements in the south west, Edward was ready to counter with another concerted offensive. All of his armies moved in at once.

Pembroke's force, composed mainly of Welsh from the lands of Rhys ap Maredudd and the southern Marcher lordships, advanced through Ceredigion, seeking to bring the Prince to battle. They did not meet with Llywelyn, but succeeded in bringing large areas back under Royal control, while John Giffard made progress in the reconquest of Carmarthen. By September, Master Giles of St George, one of King Edward's Savoyard masons, was at Aberystwyth, repairing the ravaged castle.

An account of one incident in the late summer's fighting in Ceredigion was given by Pembroke's second-in-command, the Justice of West Wales, Robert Tibetot, in a letter to the Bishop of Bath and Wells; Philip Daubeney and the men operating from Cardigan castle had taken great booty in Cardiganshire. And Rhys ap Maredudd had found out that Gruffydd ap Maredudd of Ceredigion and his brother Cynan were at Trefilan. Therefore Rhys and Tibetot had attempted a night march, over a distance of twenty-four leagues, in an attempt to take the rebel lords by surprise. Gruffydd and Cynan had escaped, but only narrowly. Eighteen prisoners held by the brothers had been released, and 3,000 head of cattle had been captured.

Only a few horses had been lost. The account captures vividly the rapid thrusts and fluid quality that marked the war in west Wales. Further east, in the Middle March, there was little movement. Roger Mortimer was doing little more than hold his own in an unstable situation. King Edward required more than this, and on 2 September he ordered his officials to hand over to Roger's envoy £500 from the Chester treasury, 'to expedite certain special business of the king'. The cryptic phrase was ominous: more often than most great families, even those of the March, the Mortimers were engaged in double-dealing. Only a year previously Roger and Llywelyn had been sworn allies. Now the alliance was over.

It was in the north, however, that the most spectacular developments took place. Edward's seaborne force, under the command of a former Constable of Gascony, Luke de Tany, succeeded in establishing itself on the island of Anglesey, which was soon brought under Royal control: the rebels had lost their granary, and they had lost the chief court of their leader, at Aberffraw. Secure on his island base, Luke de Tany began to build a bridge of boats across the Menai Strait, which would enable him to cross to Bangor and strike at the mainland bases of the Prince. Large numbers of carpenters were shipped out to him from Edward's headquarters at Rhuddlan, and the bridge rapidly took shape.

Meanwhile, the King, with the bulk of the northern forces, advanced through the lands east of the Conwy: in September Ruthin was taken, and Denbigh fell in the following month. This steady advance, which by the autumn had brought the Royal forces to the banks of the Conwy and the very edge of Snowdonia, had the effect of bringing Llywelyn back from the south to aid his brother in the defence of the mountain stronghold. The Prince's departure eased the task of the King's commanders in the south, where John Giffard was able to bring Carmarthen speedily into subjection.

Already the lands of the rebels were being shared out among the victors: in Ceredigion the possessions of Gruffydd ap Maredudd and his brother Cynan were made over by the King to Rhys ap Maredudd, who also received territories which had belonged to Rhys Wyndod in Ystrad Tywi. To the north, Roger Mortimer the younger was granted the lands around Chirk which had been held by Llywelyn Fychan; the Earl of Warenne took the territories of Llywelyn Fychan's brother Gruffydd, and his nephews Gruffydd and Llywelyn, sons of Madog, in Bromfield and Ial. Reginald de Grey was given the area around Ruthin, and the Earl of Lincoln acquired a substantial lordship based on Denbigh.

Clearly the political map of Wales was being decisively re-drawn. But no finality was possible while Snowdonia remained unpenetrated, sheltering the Prince and his brother, and the dispossessed lords of the south and east. These were ready to sally out to wreak vengeance upon those who now occupied their lands, ordering their

44

peasantry, herding their beasts and gathering their crops. The King hesitated to risk a hasty assault on the mountain fortress. Any error in tactics now would be severely punished, for his adversaries excelled in fighting in such terrain. The prospect of a long and arduous campaign, extending through the winter, now presented itself. It was daunting: summer warfare in Wales was bad enough, for men said that when it was summer elsewhere it was like winter in Wales. And a long campaign would be expensive, for the encirclement of the rebel forces must be maintained in strength, and that meant heavy expenditure on wages.

But perhaps there might be another way of bringing the war to a conclusion. One man at least in the Royal court was urging the King to try negotiations with the rebel leaders. John Peckham, Archbishop of Canterbury, had had some experience of dealing with the Welsh, and now asked for leave to go under truce and parley with Llywelyn and his magnates. Perhaps some formula could be devised which would bring a surrender and thus spare Edward the cost of a war à outrance. Grudgingly the King agreed, and Peckham set off.

# V

# No Peace for Princes

In late October and early November a stream of proposals and counter-proposals, complaints and refutations of complaints, flowed between Peckham and the Welsh leaders. The opening exchanges were pure rhetoric. Peckham declared that he had heard that the Welsh were behaving worse than the Saracens; these latter, if they captured Christians, at least kept them alive so that they might be ransomed; the Welsh, however, killed their captives, as if blood alone would satisfy them. Worse still, they were said to accept ransoms for captives, who were then handed over dead. Not so, replied the Prince; it was the English and their allies who were bloodthirsty, as the facts clearly proved, for they spared not sex, age or infirmity, nor did they respect churches and sacred places; the Welsh did not do such things. If they had done, could they be blamed? The Welsh were oppressed, ground under foot, plundered and reduced to servitude by the Royal officials, more severely, indeed, than if they had been Saracens or Jews. Though they had complained often to the King, they could obtain no help; he simply sent even more vicious and harsh officials; and when these were satiated by their own cruelties, fresh ones were sent to torment the people, who had reached the point at which they preferred death to life on such terms.

Then came the detailed statements of grievances from the Welsh side: from the men of the northern districts, Rhos, Ystrad Alun, Penllyn, and Tegeingl; from the Welsh lords, Rhys Wyndod, Llywelyn and Hywel, sons of Rhys; Gruffydd and Cynan, sons of Maredudd, Llywelyn Fychan, Goronwy ap Heilyn, the lord Dafydd and the Prince himself.

Peckham took their protestations seriously; he humbly asked the King to take heed of them: they did much to excuse the excesses of the Welsh. Edward's reply was arch: the misdeeds of the rebels were inexcusable; and as for their claim that they could not get justice, he had always been prepared to show justice to anyone. Again Peckham pleaded, and this time Edward softened a little: he would hear the complaints.

Peckham hastened back into Snowdonia to meet Llywelyn. The Prince professed himself willing to submit to Edward, on two conditions: he would do nothing against his conscience, by which he was bound to aid his people: and he would do nothing which would infringe his dignity as a Prince. Edward received this news coldly: there could be no peace unless Llywelyn and his followers put themselves entirely at his mercy, without condition.

The Archbishop was perplexed, for his moves for peace seemed to have come to nought. Yet he made one final effort to secure agreement between the two sides. He obtained the King's permission to confer with the magnates of the court, and together they drew up a peace plan to be offered to the Prince and his men. It was a classic exercise in face-saving: Edward would not be seen to be making concessions in advance of the rebels' submission, but Llywelyn and Dafydd would nevertheless receive guarantees that their treatment at the King's hands would not be too severe. In order to achieve this, two sets of proposals were drawn up by Peckham, the first to be put to Llywelyn in public, and the second in secret. The former were uncompromising: the King would dispose of North Wales as he thought fit, and Llywelyn must submit unconditionally in the hope that Edward would deal mercifully with him and his people.

The secret articles went into rather more detail. If Llywelyn would submit, he could hope for an English earldom worth £1,000 per year, in return for giving up North Wales to the King; Edward would provide for the Prince's daughter; and if Llywelyn should marry again and produce a son, the King might permit him to succeed to the earldom. The King would provide honourably and kindly for the people of North Wales. The proposals put to Dafydd required him to go on crusade to the Holy Land, never to return unless permitted to do so by the King; Edward would provide for his children.

These, then, were the inducements which were to bring Llywelyn and Dafydd to submission: personal safety — though of a precarious kind in Dafydd's case — and a degree of material security, in return for the renunciation of the land of their ancestors. But however attractive or otherwise such proposals might be to the brothers, they had had personal experience of the way in which the English honoured such agreements. Back in the 1240s, after the death of their grandfather Llywelyn the Great, their father Gruffydd had been imprisoned by their uncle David, who seized the whole Principality of North Wales for himself. Gruffydd's wife and a group of her friends among the Welsh and Marcher lords had paid King Henry III large sums of money to secure his release and restore him to a share of the Principality. But when Henry forced David to hand Gruffydd over, he simply placed him in custody in the Tower of London, along with his sons

Owain and Dafydd. There Gruffydd had remained for three years, until on St David's Day, 1244, he tried to escape by climbing down a rope improvised from his sheets and clothes. The makeshift rope broke, and Gruffydd was killed in the fall. Who was to say that a similar sequence of betrayals was not now waiting for Gruffydd's sons?

The replies to the proposals, sent by Llywelyn and Dafydd to Peckham on 11 November, mark the difference in character between the two brothers. The Prince was dignified. The proposals tended more to the ruin and destruction of him and his people than to their honour and security, and therefore his council would in no wise allow him to accept them, even had he wished to do so, and the other nobles and people subject to him would not agree to proposals which involved their undoubted destruction.

Dafydd was contemptuous and insulting in his reply: when he wished to go to the Holy Land, he would do so of his own free will, for the sake of God, not of any man. The Prince and his men were fighting the just war, for the defence of their own, and God would aid them against the King's forces, who committed sacrilege, and showed no mercy to priests, monks, the blind, the deaf, the dumb, to children nor to the infirm of either sex; let Peckham turn his censure against those who did wrong.

This stung Peckham into a final, bitter rejoinder. He had done all that he could in the interests of peace, at considerable personal risk. He was in no mood to be lectured to, and he launched into a savage attack on Welsh history and custom. Llywelyn had claimed to hold North Wales by right of descent from Brutus the Trojan, whose followers were traditionally held to be the progenitors of the Welsh people. Now Peckham turned this tradition against the Prince: the Trojans who were alleged to have settled in Britain had only done so because they had been driven from their homeland for supporting the adulterous Paris. Their vile ways were reflected in the Welsh laws, which respected marriage so little that bastards were accorded full rights of succession, contrary to the dictates of the Scriptures. It was no more than a just retribution for their sins and their usurpation of Britain that the Welsh had been pushed out of most of the land by the Anglo-Saxons. And now the Welsh were so deeply sunk into barbarism that the world would not know that they even existed, were it not for the fact that a few of them were to be found begging in France. They had said that God would help them. It was to be hoped, returned Peckham grimly, that He would.

The Archbishop's letter was written on 14 November, and at its close he reminded the rebels that if they should come to their senses and wish to seek peace, they would always find him ready to help. But by then events had overtaken the Archbishop's quest for an end to the fighting, and the Prince and his men were once more in buoyant mood.

# VI

# *Death Turns the Tide*

By late October, the time spent on the island of Anglesey was beginning to drag for men like Peter de la Mare, one of the knights in Luke de Tany's occupying army. The weather was turning colder, and the great peaks of Snowdonia, frowning down from across the Menai Straits, emphasised the remoteness and hostility of the place in which Peter now found himself, far from his Northamptonshire lands at Maxey and Northburgh, which he held as a tenant of the Abbot of Peterborough, and where he had left his wife Christiana and young son Geoffrey.

Disquiet of a different kind was in the mind of one of Peter's companions, Hywel ap Gruffydd. Hywel was indeed much more at home on Anglesey: his family had held land on the island for three generations. Yet as one of the influential men of north Wales who had long ago taken the side of Edward I, Hywel had good reason to feel apprehensive about the fighting which would follow the army's crossing of the Menai. For among the men who would face him he could expect to find near kinsmen of his. His brother Rhys was with the King, it is true, but there were cousins who still held to Llywelyn. For Hywel this was a civil war.

And then there were men who looked forward to the

crossing of the Menai as an opportunity to settle old scores. One such was Roger Clifford the younger, son of the man of the same name who had been captured and grievously wounded in Dafydd's attack on Hawarden Castle in March.

For some time the troops had done little but wait, as the carpenters and sailors worked on the bridge of boats over which the knights would lead the move to the mainland. But all must wait until Luke de Tany had word from Edward. The next attack in the north was to be two-pronged, with de Tany crossing the Menai as Edward's men burst across the Conwy. The Welsh defending the route along the coast would be attacked front and rear, and should be overwhelmed.

Still the prospect of the crossing made men nervous: most would rather have that dangerous manoeuvre behind them. Luke de Tany chafed like the rest, when at the beginning of November, he sensed an opportunity to get his men across, and to win no small glory for himself. For the moment the Welsh were distracted by the deep negotiations with Archbishop Peckham, a few miles along the coast to the east, at Aber. With their attention focussed on peace-talks, they would hardly expect a sudden move from Anglesey. Perhaps this was a chance to end the whole struggle quickly. De Tany had, moreover, made contacts among the Welsh on the mainland, particularly among the clergy at Bangor, who had promised to aid him. They would give a signal to show when the time for a crossing was opportune.

On 6 November the signal came, after de Tany's accomplices had had a secret meeting in the bell-tower of Bangor Cathedral. De Tany's men began to push across the bridge of boats, until some hundreds of them were near the mainland. With the leaders rode Peter de la Mare, Hywel ap Gruffydd and Roger Clifford.

Something went wrong. In the hills the Prince's men were alerted, and they poured down to the attack. There was great confusion, and to de Tany's force retreat seemed the only course open. But under the press of men the bridge began to give way. Men and horses were thrown into the water, and the knights, weighted down by their armour, were helpless. They died, not honourably, facing their enemies, but drowning, as the encasing metal dragged them down under the waters of the Menai.|Luke de Tany was among the dead, as was Roger Clifford. Among the widows made that day was Gwenhwyfar, wife of Hywel ap Gruffydd: she was to receive ten marks of the King's gift for her losses in the war. And soon the Abbot of Peterborough was arranging for the wardship of Geoffrey de la Mare, when it was sure that his father, too, had drowned. A dozen others of knightly rank, a score of cavalry, and some hundreds of foot soldiers were lost in the disaster. Not all of the Bangor clergy had turned against the Prince; one of the canons, Madog Fychan, was among those who had descended on Luke de Tany's men, and with his own hands dragged a horseman from the saddle to his death.

The effect on the Royal forces was instantaneous. The remainder of the Anglesey army was stranded on the island, quite incapable of launching an attack until it was reinforced and the bridge rebuilt. And without their support the King would not contemplate advancing over the Conwy. At once he pulled his headquarters back to Rhuddlan, from where he could superintend the sending of carpenters (sixty of whom were re-employed) and fresh troops to Anglesey. Before the long-contemplated assault on Snowdonia was made, both organisation and morale would have to be restored.

Among the followers of Llywelyn, the battle at the

Menai produced predictable exultation. There was no chance now of a surrender, such as had been suggested by Peckham, when the Prince was being assured by all those around him that he must be the leader who, as had been prophesied by the Welsh seers, would one day wear the crown of Brutus on his head in London itself.

After the defeat of de Tany's men, there was indeed little purpose in Llywelyn's holding back from a further attack on the King's forces. But where was it to be made? An attempt to re-conquer Anglesey required more sea-power than Llywelyn could muster; a direct attack on the large Royal forces grouped around the King himself east of the Conwy would be suicidal. A renewed sally into west Wales was possible — but already Edward, in anticipation of this threat, was calling up reinforcements into that area. One region remained in which there had not yet been a major campaign: the central and southern March.

An assault on the March was attractive for many reasons. In the first place the Welsh of the area might prove easy to raise in rebellion, for they would not be war-weary, and would not have experienced the sobering impact of large numbers of Edward's soldiery. Again, many districts in the March had been under Llywelyn's direct control until only five years ago: before 1277 Southern Powys, Ceri, Cydewain, Builth, Brecon, Gwerthrynion and Elfael, almost the entire Welsh borderland, had been in the Prince's hands, governed by bailiffs directly appointed by him. This had given the Prince close contacts with the leading men of the Marcher districts, and a particularly personal call upon their loyalty.

Most significantly, however, late October had seen the death of Edward's commander in this central and southern sector, Roger Mortimer. Mortimer's death was of great interest to Llywelyn. The lord of Wigmore was succeeded as commander of the King's forces in central Wales by Roger Lestrange of Knockin. In some respects this was a shrewd appointment: successful Royal operations in this central sector would depend largely on the co-operation of the leading Welsh lord of the area, Gruffydd ap Gwenwynwyn of Southern Powys; and whereas Gruffydd had been in conflict with Roger Mortimer over territories claimed by them both, with the Lestranges he enjoyed much better relations. His wife, Hawise, was a sister of Roger Lestrange, and the family were old allies of Gruffydd in the complex pattern of feuds which had regularly disrupted the life of the March. Lestrange, however, was not the figure that Mortimer had been: in an area where the barons were notoriously touchy about their dignity, it was quite possible that he would find it hard to assert his authority over the magnates allegedly under his orders.

Mortimer had been a powerful figure — the greatest landholder of the Middle March, celebrated for his largesse, and to his Welsh tenantry no alien figure, for he was the son of Gwladus Ddu, daughter of Llywelyn the Great. He was thus the cousin of Llywelyn ap Gruffydd. Such a man could be expected to keep the March in order. But after his death, confusion reigned. He had left large debts to the King, which were to be settled by his heirs, and this involved potentially lengthy negotiations, during which the Mortimer lands and tenants would be without a lord. And lordless men could not be trusted: there was no knowing to whom they might turn for leadership. The King's officials in the areas near to Mortimer's territories were clearly worried by the situation.

Roger Springhose, Sheriff of Shropshire, was ordered by the King to take control of Mortimer's lands and castles, and to try to keep the tenantry loyal. But when he went to carry out these orders, Springhose found all manner of problems; it proved impossible to collect revenue from the Welsh of Mortimer's lordship: the country was not yet pacified. At the castle of Clun, the Sheriff and his fellow-officials had installed a Constable, Thomas de la Hyde, to command in the King's name. While they were talking to Thomas outside the walls, however, the garrison locked them out. The men of the castle were apparently unimpressed by commands uttered in the King's name: they regarded themselves as loyal to Maud, Roger Mortimer's widow, who was clearly displeased by the intervention of the Royal officers in her late husband's lands.

Still more ominously Springhose reported that, though he had done his best to induce the people of those lands to be loyal to the King, and had spent much money in setting the castles in good order, he found the inhabitants very fickle and haughty, as though on the point of leaving the King's peace, because they had no definite lord. He requested urgently that 'the business of the heir' should be settled as quickly as possible. Accordingly, on 24 November, Edward placed Edmund, Roger Mortimer's eldest son, in formal possession of his father's lands. The tenants once more had a Mortimer as their lord. But his authority over them would not for long remain unchallenged. For the rumour began to spread that Prince Llywelyn had left Snowdonia.

# VII

# *The Last Battle*

Llywelyn had indeed struck south-east. It was not long before his trail was picked up by the waiting Royal commanders. Late in November, Roger Lestrange was composing a routine letter of report to the King. He had been visiting the areas of his command, trying to settle the disturbed state of the March. He had been ordered to attack the enemy, but they were sheltering beyond the Berwyn mountains, terrain so repellent that he could not enter it without endangering his men, which the King had forbidden. (Clearly Edward was resolved not to permit any more precipitate advances such as had brought Luke de Tany to defeat). Lestrange's letter began to tail off: requests for the King to order various Marcher magnates to prevent the passage of supplies to the enemy: a sign perhaps of sympathy for Llywelyn among the Welsh of the March. But suddenly, an excited postcript: as the letter was being written, news had come in that Llywelyn had entered Southern Powys, the land of Gruffydd ap Gwenwynwyn. Lestrange hastily made ready to intercept him.

He was able to collect the forces stationed at Montgomery and Oswestry, while he could count on aid from the lord of Southern Powys, from the Mortimers in the middle and northern March, and from the troops at Builth Castle, under John Giffard. For his part Llywelyn

57

was rousing the discontented elements in every district through which he passed: Southern Powys, particularly Cyfeiliog and Arwystli, which he claimed as rightfully his, contained many who would join him. By the early days of December he was close to Maelienydd, whence some of the fickle tenantry of the Mortimers might be added to the host: and then into Gwerthrynion, a district which for many years had been part of his own lands, until it too was seized by the Mortimers after the last war.

In the second week of December, the Prince was in the locality of the Abbey of Cwm Hir. This was one of the Cistercian houses of Wales, whose monks had long been among Llywelyn's most steadfast supporters. But Cwm Hir was no place in which to linger: the peace of its precincts called temptingly to the aged leader, but his need was to press forward and carry war through the March, to confound his enemies and give heart to his friends. On the morning of Friday, 11 December, therefore, Llywelyn and his army moved out of Gwerthrynion and into the land of Builth, a hilly region where John Giffard held Builth castle for the King, at the confluence of the rivers Irfon and Wye.

It was not a landscape which brought comfort to the fainthearted, marked as it was by sudden dips in the hills and by mist-filled valleys in which many an ambush might be laid.

They had been joined by some of the local magnates, including Rhys ap Gruffydd, once the Prince's steward of Builth in the days when Llewelyn had been lord of that land.

At Llanganten, a few miles to the west of the town of Builth, the Prince halted his forces and made the decision to divide them. Some were to go on, under the command of Dafydd ab Einion Fychan, the Prince's steward, to gather support in Brecon. The remainder, under Llywelyn, were beginning to move towards Builth when they were confronted by the advance units of Lestrange's army.

We shall never know what was in Llywelyn's mind at this time. He must have known that Lestrange's forces were close to him, but if he was planning a confrontation, then the division of his own army at Llanganten would seem to bespeak a foolhardy over-confidence. It may be, however, that the Prince was acting under a delusion as to his adversaries' strength and intentions. Welsh and English stories about this day refer repeatedly to treachery, and the Mortimer brothers are frequently mentioned by contemporary chroniclers as having lured Llywelyn into danger. There is no proof, but much suspicion. For the Prince was certainly carrying on this day a letter, in which the identity of men was concealed by false names, but in which many of the Marcher lords, and others, might be identified. Its contents seemed to reveal disunity and disloyalty amongst the Royal forces. For years the sudden changing of sides and the launching of treacherous assaults had characterised warfare in the Welsh March. Had Llywelyn now been duped into believing that some of his adversaries were prepared to desert their comrades?

Whatever his hopes, the Prince's disposition of his men betrays no hint of slackness. Lestrange and his troops were approaching from the east, on the south side of the river Irfon. Against them, Llywelyn ranged the bulk of his forces on a hill overlooking, to the north, the river Wye, with a smaller contingent sent forward to the south to hold a bridge over the Irfon, close to the point at which it ran into the Wye. With the two rivers interposed between them, there seemed no chance that the two armies would come rapidly to grips. And so they stood, deadlocked, and stared at each other.

With Lestrange were almost all of the leading lords and Royal officials of the Middle March: John Giffard, Constable of Builth; the sons of Roger Mortimer; two of the sons of Gruffydd ap Gwenwynwyn of Powys; John Lestrange of Knockin; Peter Corbet, lord of Caus; Reginald fitz Peter, lord of Talgarth in Brycheiniog, together with men from further afield, like Simon Basset of Sapcote, and Ralph Basset of Drayton, in Staffordshire. It was not an easy force to lead, for its ranks were riven by age-old jealousies. Gruffydd ap Gwenwynwyn and his sons were ancient foes of the Corbets and more recently, of the Mortimers; for decades a Corbet-Lestrange feud had been virulent. There was much to feed hopes in Llywelyn that his enemies might turn on each other. Only a year previously he had made a treaty of peace and mutual aid with Roger Mortimer. No common adversary was named, but it was almost certainly directed against Gruffydd ap Gwenwynwyn, with whom both men had important disputes over land.

But the Prince's own force was scarcely more compact. As well as Llywelyn's own troops, there were men from Ceredigion, local levies under Rhys ap Gruffydd, and men from Northern Powys led by Llywelyn Fychan. Llywelyn Fychan, lord of Cynllaith and Nanheudwy, must have hungered for the battle as he faced across the Irfon that afternoon. His ancestral lands had already been overrun by Royal forces, and given by King Edward as a gift to the young Roger Mortimer. Now the two rival lords of Chirk were but a few hundred yards distant. A bitterness lay in Llywelyn Fychan against others of those who now confronted him: in the months before the outbreak of war the sons of Gruffydd ap Gwenwynwyn and the men of Roger Lestrange himself had seized him on the road to Chester and held him captive until he had bought his freedom. Now came the time to avenge that humiliation.

As the afternoon wore on, however, it seemed that there would be no fighting that day. So confident of this was the Prince that he slipped away from his army with only a few attendants. To scout for a way of attacking Lestrange? To raise more local support? To make secret contact with those whom he thought his allies among the opposing forces? To check the state of his outposts — particularly the one guarding the bridge over the Irfon? It cannot be known, but whatever the reason, Llywelyn was not with his men when the Royal army made its next, and decisive move.

Lestrange had sought out a local man of English stock, one Helias Walwyn, who knew a ford across the Irfon, and would guide the Royal troops to it. Thus as dusk began to fall, the men despatched by Llywelyn to guard the Irfon bridge suddenly found a party of English troops bearing down on them from the flanks. A short struggle, and the bridge was in Lestrange's hands; his men poured across and began to advance up the hill towards the Prince's army.

Llywelyn's men stood firm, and the northerners among them hurled their javelins, their traditional weapons, among the oncoming warriors. But they were leaderless and shocked, and now grievously harassed by the archers brought up to face them, while cavalry began to work round their flanks. As the sky darkened, the fighting grew confused, a series of scattered encounters, with much slaughter.

Somewhere on the edge of this untidy battlefield, Stephen Frankton led a contingent of horsemen, looking for groups of the Prince's soldiers. Frankton was one of Roger Lestrange's retainers, from Ellesmere in Shropshire; a tough man, experienced in the harsh ways of the Welsh borders. Now in the dusk he saw a Welshman attended by a small group of servants: some minor chief, perhaps; certainly worth despatching. He and his troop of horsemen gave chase; he came up with that man and ran him through with his lance. The Welshman fell, not dead, but terribly wounded. It was enough. Frankton rode away. He did not yet know the identity of the man whom he had struck down.

When servants of Edmund Mortimer came upon him, Llywelyn ap Gruffydd, Prince of Wales, lord of Snowdon, was not yet dead. He lived long enough to ask for a priest; none came. His men, already embroiled with the Royal army, cannot have known of his death. Even had they contrived to turn back Lestrange's force, no victory could now have been theirs. As it was they fell, not fully realising the futility of their fight. Some told of the death of all of Llywelyn's cavalry, 160 strong, and of three thousand out of seven thousand foot-soldiers. Among the dead was Rhys ap Gruffydd of Builth. And Roger Mortimer's possession of Chirk would no more be troubled by the claims of Llywelyn Fychan, for he too lay among the slain.

The official report of the action was sent to Edward, encamped in the north, by Roger Lestrange. Its brevity betrays the satisfaction of a man who has deserved well of his master.

'Know, sire, that the forces that you placed under my command fought with Llywelyn ap Gruffydd in the land of Builth on Friday after the feast of St Nicholas, and that Llywelyn ap Gruffydd is dead, his army broken, and all the flower of his men killed, as the bearer of this letter will tell you.'

With the report was sent a more signal mark of the victory: the Prince's head was cut off and carried to the King, for the encouragement of his troops.

The followers of the dead Prince needed no sight of his severed head to remind them of their loss, but his poet, Gruffydd ab yr Ynad Coch, saw the ghastly spectacle, and the sight nearly broke him.

'It is small gain to me, only deception, that my head is left me when he has lost his; when that head was cut off, men welcomed terror; when that head was cut off, it was better to submit. The head of a warrior, ever to be praised, of a champion, of a hero, was his; the head of Llywelyn the fair, it is woe to the world that an iron stake has pierced it; the head of my lord, the torment of his grievous fall is upon me; the head of my life, without a name; the head which owned the homage of nine hundred lands, and which had nine hundred feasts; the head of a prince who showered iron spears, the head of a proud hawk-prince who breached the battle-line, the head of a princely plunging wolf, may the princely Head of Heaven be his protection.'

The sense of loss was almost too great to bear:

'Oh God, that the sea might surge up, and cover the land; why are we left to linger?'

The anguish of the Welsh poet was thrown into contrast by the mockery of an Englishman, Peter Langtoft, whose verse chronicle contained the bitter jest

'Llywelyn has been shamefully decapitated: he has no need of a hat.'

Indeed, it had not been a heroic death: almost alone, in an unregarded corner of the battlefield, lured there by who knew what manner of treacherous promises? The Welsh chroniclers passed over it quickly: if any on the Welsh side knew what had happened, none carried the tale from the battlefield. Anyway, silence was politic. Nor did any of the English chroniclers give a clear account of the killing, though returning soldiers carried their partial and confused stories around the country. On December

63

evenings the mist hangs heavy in the Irfon valley, and the dusk comes quickly. Perhaps no-one really knew what had happened. But curiously no-one seemed to want to claim the credit for the Prince's death, or to proclaim his part in it.

But the indignities were not yet over. After being shown to the northern army, the Prince's head was carried to London, where it was exhibited on the Tower of London for the gratification of the populace. In derision, it was crowned with a circlet of ivy. Crowned in London: the prophesy of the Welsh seers was thus grimly fulfilled.

The fate of the Prince's corpse was more seemly. After Archbishop Peckham had been satisfied that Llywelyn had died penitent, he allowed it to be carried away by the monks of Cwm Hir, one of whom had sung mass for the Prince on the morning of the battle. Somewhere in the abbey cemetery, the body of Llywelyn ap Gruffydd was given decent burial.

And meanwhile, the news of the death was spread abroad. In Italy, one of Edward's clerks, Master Stephen of St George, heard of it, and wrote exultantly of the killing of 'that old serpent, the father of treachery, the child of rebellion, the son of iniquity, the author of sedition, the patron of ingratitude, convict of perjury, head of all evil'.

# VIII

# *The Hunt for Dafydd*

With the death of Llywelyn and the breaking of his southern army, the military balance swung decisively in favour of the King.

To the west, there was some success for Edward's opponents in Ceredigion as the year closed. Patrick de Chaworth, at the head of Royal forces brought up from Kidwelly, suddenly and ominously disappears from the records, while one of the King's captains in the west, Roger Mortimer, lost his horse, worth 20 marks, in fighting in Glyn Aeron. But William de Valence was at work gathering a force of about 1,500 men for a new campaign and, within a few weeks, had advanced to Aberystwyth, where Roger Mortimer of west Wales was installed as Constable of the castle.

The disaster at the Menai was now forgotten: the morale of the Royal forces was as greatly boosted as that of the rebels was shattered. Dafydd, in truth, had the prize for which he had plotted in 1274, for he was chosen by the rebel magnates to succeed his brother as Prince of Wales. But his new dignity rang more than hollow: he was lord of a principality which consisted of little more than Snowdonia, and was hemmed in by Royal forces growing stronger by the day. And there were many in Gwynedd who had stood by Llywelyn but would not be prepared to fight for the renegade Dafydd.

Nor could Dafydd hope that the bitterness of the Welsh winter would deter Edward from pressing home his attack. Even before Llywelyn's death, the King had issued writs for the levying of more soldiers. On the day after Llywelyn was struck down, Edward, as yet unaware of the course of events in the south, was overseeing the provisioning of the Anglesey army: corn, salt, flour, iron and nails were to be shipped to the island as soon as possible. Edward was preparing for a winter campaign, and he was resolved not to leave its direction to subordinates. Ten days after the battle of the Irfon, he sent out orders to have tents and pavilions brought up from Chester to Rhuddlan, together with timber and carpenters, so that a proper supply of tent-poles could be made. Two hundred of the poles were to be bound with iron, for the setting up of the Royal chamber and chapel. So the King was going to keep his Christmas in the field.

A few days later, another mandate revealed that this season had seen a decisive advance by the Anglesey army. Edward ordered that two smiths, with 16,000 large nails for making palisades, should be shipped to Bangor. Clearly the Anglesey troops had crossed the Menai and secured a foothold on the mainland.

Now Edward began to move his headquarters westwards, up to the east bank of the Conwy. The river was crossed in the New Year, and Dafydd's square-towered castle of Dolwyddelan was beseiged. It had fallen by the end of January, and its custody was entrusted by the King to a man from Gwynedd, Gruffydd ap Tudur. Gruffydd's family were old servants of the Princes, but his future and that of his progeny lay in the Royal service. In Edward's train was Rhodri ap Gruffydd. Men must have viewed him with curiosity. He was the youngest brother of Prince Llywelyn. His life had been spent as a pawn in the great struggles between Llywelyn and the English kings. Handed over to the latter as a hostage for his brother's good behaviour, abandoned to whatever fate they might have in mind for him, forced to renounce his rights in the Principality in return for Llywelyn's promise of 1,000 marks, a promise not honoured, Rhodri was of little account. He would survive·this war, and live out his life on the English manors which he acquired through his marriages and through scraps of Royal favour. His grandson, Owain Lawgoch, Owain of the Bloody Hand, would revive a claim to the Principality of Wales, would take service with England's enemies, the French, and plot the invasion of Wales. The government of King Edward's grandson would pay him the compliment of taking him seriously enough to arrange for his assassination by his own squire. But that was far in the future. Now, as a faithful subject of King Edward, Rhodri ap Gruffydd was assisting in the remorseless assault on his brothers.

Edward I was now ready to begin the close encirclement of Snowdonia. Soon his troops held all the western bank of the river Conwy, down to its estuary, while the Anglesey army under Otto de Grandison worked round the coast westwards from Bangor, occupying Caernarfon before pressing south to Harlech. In desperation Dafydd moved his entourage into the heart of Snowdonia, though it was now all too easily penetrated by the formidable Gascons, who were arriving in growing strength. To the south, the army of west Wales under William de Valence and the central Wales forces of Roger Lestrange were advancing on the stronghold of Castell y Bere. Perhaps the most spectacular of the castles built by the thirteenth-century princes, Bere perches grandly on the slopes of Cader Idris. It was perfectly placed for a heroic resistance, but no great struggle took place. The King's forces approached Bere in strength in mid-April. On 22 April Cynfrig ap Madog, Dafydd's Constable of the castle, and six of his fellow-defenders, entered into a formal agreement with Valence and Lestrange. They sold Castell y Bere to the King's men. The price was £80. Four days later the transfer was complete: from the 'rock of Bere', Valence sent out orders for victuals to be sent up for the use of his garrison. Placed in command was another Welshman, whose Frenchified name of Lewis de la Pole conceals the identity of Llywelyn, one of the sons of Gruffydd ap Gwenwynwyn, lord of Southern Powys. That wily old magnate, who had fought against three generations of the house of Gwynedd, was now enjoying, and materially assisting in, the downfall of its members.

There remained but one castle which Dafydd could make his base: that was Dolbadarn, crowning the Llanberis pass in Snowdonia. Here, at the start of May, in the great round tower, Dafydd assembled the magnates who still held to him. Gruffydd ap Maredudd of Ceredigion was with the Prince, though his brother Cynan had given up the struggle and surrendered; Hywel ap Rhys Gryg of Ystrad Tywi was there, as were Rhys Wyndod, Llywelyn ap Rhys of Is Cennen, Rhys Fychan ap Rhys ap Maelgwn, and Morgan ap Maredudd. Here was the defiant remnant of the formidable army of Welsh lords who had confronted the King's men the year before.

It was a strange atmosphere that prevailed at Dolbadarn in those early summer days. Dafydd and his followers were living a kind of fantasy. On 2 May, Gruffydd ap Maredudd made, and Dafydd confirmed, a solemn grant to Rhys Fychan. He made over to him the land of Penweddig in northern Ceredigion. The condition was that Rhys would agree to bring all his forces to Dafydd whenever the Prince should demand them, before 24

June. But Ceredigion was firmly in Royal hands; Rhys had few or no forces to bring to anyone; and they would all be lucky still to be at liberty by 24 June.

In the same vein, and on the same day, Dafydd gave to one John, son of David, special powers to call out the men of Brecon, Builth, Maelienydd, Elfael, Gwerthrynion and Ceri, 'as if we were present'. John took with him documents bearing the call to arms; the men of the named districts were to take heed of these documents, because the envoy dared not take letters personally to each area. So Dafydd was planning a campaign in the Middle March, such as the one which had resulted in Llywelyn's death. But Llywelyn had taken an army through that land before he was killed; all Dafydd could send was a lone envoy who dared not visit the districts which he was calling out to war. There were, it seems, still insurgents in the Middle March but, in a letter to Edmund Mortimer, the King dismissed them as thieves lurking in the woods, and ordered Edmund to get rid of them. This was the state of things when John son of David set off on his mission. He was never heard of again. Already the King's men were staking their claims to territories much closer to Dafydd's base than those to which he had sent John, son of David. Roger Lestrange had let it be known that he would like Penllyn and Edeirnion, on the edge of Gwynedd itself, or perhaps Maelor Saesneg on the north-east border of Wales.

And the widening swathes which were being cut through the forestlands of eastern Wales ensured that Royal forces would pour unhindered into the country, to quash any revival of Dafydd's fortunes. On the day when the Prince was issuing his meaningless charters and letters of summons, thirteen hundred men under Reginald de Grey were clearing the pass of Bodfari, between Ruthin and Rhuddlan.

Now the English could talk of Dafydd's 'playing the fox': he was no more than a fugitive, with small bands of soldiery out scouring the hills for him. These were not cumbersome groups of heavily armed men, vulnerable to the attacks with which Dafydd might have harassed such warriors, but slightly-armed, fast-moving groups, often composed of Welsh from the March, or of local Welshmen lured into Royal service by the promise of reward. For fear and greed combined to make many men anxious to please the King. On 25 June, Edward issued a grant of freedom from military service beyond eastern Gwynedd to a group of Welshmen from that land, Einion ab Ifor and Goronwy ap Dafydd and their sons. God's clemency, wrote the King, had so visited him that when he was lately at Aberconwy (in mid-June) these Welshmen had brought to him part of the wood of the True Cross, called by the Welsh, Croes Naid, which had been owned by Llywelyn ap Gruffydd, late Prince of Wales, and his ancestors. The sacred relic was later carried in solemn procession through London, and lodged in St George's Chapel, Windsor, where it was carefully tended for centuries.

Other Welshmen brought in to the King a jewel which they called the crown of Arthur, probably the coronet which the princes of the north wore on ceremonial occasions. But a grander prize also fell into the King's hands. Dafydd himself was captured. On 28 June, Edward was able to issue writs of summons to a Parliament at Shrewsbury on the morrow of Michaelmas, at which those present would discuss the fate of Dafydd, brother of Llywelyn ap Gruffydd. The two brothers had, as was well known, burned the King's towns, killed many of his subjects, imprisoned others, and attacked the King's castles. 'But God, wishing to put an end to these evil proceedings, has after the death of Llywelyn, destined

Dafydd, the last survivor of that family of traitors, to the King's prison, after he has been captured by men of his own race'.

With Dafydd had been taken his wife Elizabeth, his daughters, and his two sons, Llywelyn and Owain. The boys were sent for safe-keeping to Bristol castle. Llywelyn died within a few years, but Owain's captivity was long. Over two decades later, King Edward still showed himself concerned lest Owain should escape, for in October of 1305 he sent a sharply worded order to the Constable of the castle:

'As the King wills that Owain son of Dafydd ap Gruffydd, who is in the Constable's custody in the castle, should be kept in future more securely than he has been previously, he orders the Constable to cause a strong house within the castle to be repaired as soon as possible, and to make a wooden cage bound with iron in that house, in which Owain may be enclosed at night.'

Owain did not escape; he is heard of no more.

The daughters of Dafydd, together with Llywelyn's only child, the infant Gwenllian were sent to be brought up in English Gilbertine nunneries. At Sempringham, in the far off fens of Lincolnshire, Gwenllian lived, supported by a Royal pension of £20 per year, until her death over half a century later.

Dafydd himself was taken at first to Rhuddlan, then sent on to Shrewsbury, to await the formality of the proceedings in the Parliament. The assembly met on 3 September, and on 30 September, Dafydd was condemned. He could not have expected mercy, for his betrayal of the trust which Edward had placed in him offended most grievously the sensibilities of the age. Writing some twenty years later, Dante was to picture the reservation of the most horrible torments of Hell for those who betrayed their lords. Whatever his fate in after-life, Dafydd now suffered punishment as hideous as any devised by the Florentine. He was dragged by horses through the streets of Shrewsbury, and at the High Cross he was hanged, and the entrails were ripped from his body. His corpse was then quartered, the quarters being sent for display to Bristol, York, Northampton, and Winchester. The representatives of the citizens of York and Winchester engaged in a grotesque dispute, as to which of the two cities should have the honour of receiving the right shoulder; it was adjudged to Winchester, and the burgesses of that place returned home well satisfied with their victory. Dafydd's head was sent to London, to be set up on the White Tower, next to that of his brother.

No legend grew; no bard lamented as Gruffydd ab yr Ynad Coch had done for Llywelyn. It was perhaps considered appropriate that one who had changed his allegiance so often should be taken by his compatriots. Even in death, Dafydd did not rival his elder brother: it was Llywelyn's head that was picked out by the Londoners as a landmark. How long he had coveted Llywelyn's princely title perhaps even Dafydd did not know: but it was his bitter fate to obtain it only when the Principality of Wales was in its death-agony, already with the life draining from it, after the lunge of Stephen Frankton's lance on that winter's day of 1282.

# Irfon Bridge —
## Matters of Fact

The account of the battle given in Chapter VII rests heavily upon the evidence of the Peterborough chronicle, much of which was printed by Thomas Stapleton, *Chronicon Petroburgense*, Camden Society, 1849, the original manuscript being Society of Antiquaries MS. 60. The account given there is reflected in outline in the Dunstable annals, (printed by H.R. Luard, (ed.), *Annales Monastici*, III Rolls Series, 1866) and it seems to me that these two sources are based on the account of an English participant in the wars, who may have visited both Dunstable and Peterborough. The Peterborough account is of value principally for its evidence on the time of the battle, the previous movements of the Prince's force, and the participants on both sides. Additional information on the events of the battle is to be found in the work of the Yorkshire chronicler, Walter of Guisborough, printed in Harry Rothwell (ed.), *The Chronicle of Walter of Guisborough*, Camden Series LXXXIX, 1957, though this account is rather a 'literary' one, in which interesting details have been embellished, and perhaps distorted. Also valuable is Thomas Jones (ed.), *Brut y Tywysogyon, Peniarth MS 20*, Caerdydd, 1941.

A major problem is the apparent clash of evidence between, on the one hand, the Peterborough and Dunstable accounts, which state that a major battle took place involving large forces on both sides, and on the other hand, the account of Brut y Tywysogyon, which suggests that Llywelyn had only a few men with him at the time of his death. A possible answer — and it is the one hinted at by Walter of Guisborough — is that both versions of the events contain a kernel of truth: the Prince's army may have been large, but he may have been isolated from it when he was struck down. It seems likely that he was accompanied by only a few men when he was felled: Gruffydd ab yr Ynad Coch's lament mentions, indeed, 'the killing of the eighteen', — but his choice of this number, *deunaw,* may have been decided by the needs of his rhyme-scheme in which every line ends in *aw.*

There are many possible explanations as to how the Prince had come to be detached from his forces: he may have been lured into a trap — though it is perhaps significant that no-one came forward to claim the credit for such a manoeuvre. He may have been checking his outposts — among them the force holding Irfon Bridge. If the defenders of the bridge had already been overwhelmed by the men guided by Helias Walwyn, then instead of meeting his own men, Llywelyn would have run into advancing Royal troops. On the other hand he may have attempted to slip away from the field when the victory of Lestrange's men seemed likely. It does at least seem clear that the Prince did not die in the midst of his troops in the course of the main encounter. Further than that it is difficult to go with any confidence: some chroniclers imply that the Prince fell early in the action, and others that he was struck down after the battle had been decided. But this may simply reflect the conditions of a confused encounter. Mediaeval battles were seldom tidy affairs, and events which might strike some participants as decisive might pass virtually unnoticed by others. This raises the question of apparent conflicts of evidence in the major sources for the battle, the Peterborough chronicle and that of Walter of Guisborough. I am impressed by the general reliability of the Peterborough account, but would stress that this does not imply rejection of much of Guisborough's narrative.

While it is clear that some parts of Guisborough's description of the battle are pure invention, such as the speeches which he puts into the mouth of Llywelyn, it is equally clear that he has got the basic geography correct. Brut y Tywysogyon, the Welsh Chronicle of the Princes, notes that Llywelyn halted his army at Llanganten, before the battle, and Llanganten lies between the Wye and the Irfon, the area in which Guisborough locates the Prince's forces. This also accords with the Peterborough chronicler's statement that the battle was fought at a spot between Cwm Hir and a place named Inla(n)make, in the land of Worymon (or possibly Worynion). Now the last name stands for Gwerthrynion, and it may be that Inla(n)make stands for (in) Llangamarch. Llangamarch stands about six miles to the south-west of Llanganten, and Cwm Hir a dozen miles to the north-east.

But if Guisborough got his basic geography correct, did he invent the bridge over the Irfon, the ford, and Helias Walwyn, all of them peculiar to his account? This is possible, but it seems to me that he has pointed to a perfectly credible tactical problem confronting the Royal forces. These were surely located, as his account suggests, on the south bank of the Irfon-Wye confluence, in the area dominated by the Royal castle, which they must have made their assembly point. Llywelyn's force, moving down from Cwm Hir, was surely on the hills at Llanganten, north of the Irfon and west of the Wye. I believe that the naming of the man who showed the Royal troops how to cross the Irfon and attack the defenders of the bridge is a sign that Guisborough was recording a genuine story.

The circumstances of Llywelyn's decapitation can also

be built up in some detail. Guisborough says that after Frankton had run Llywelyn through, he left him, but returned later, evidently with companions, and *they* decapitated the Prince. The 14th-century Lincolnshire chronicler, Robert Mannyng, states that one Robert Body cut off the Prince's head. Both of these distant chroniclers, Guisborough and Mannyng, have in fact preserved the names of men, Frankton and Body, who were by no means famous, yet can be traced in record sources as tenants and military companions of Roger Lestrange. One of them, Frankton, struck the Prince down, and the other, Body, cut off his head.

# Bibliography

This list is intended as a guide for the interested general reader, and so articles in learned journals are omitted, as are manuscripts and printed collections of documents in the original languages (Latin, Norman French, and Middle Welsh).

The classic work on the political history of mediaeval Wales remains J.E. Lloyd, *A History of Wales from the earliest times to the Edwardian Conquest,* London, 3rd edition, 1939. The treatment of the 1282-3 war is, however, slight. Much more detailed, particularly on the English military build-up, is J.E. Morris, *The Welsh Wars of Edward I,* Oxford, 1901. Much raw material can be found in the fascinating collection of J.G. Edwards, *A Calendar of Ancient Correspondence concerning Wales,* Cardiff, 1935. Anyone wishing to absorb the atmosphere of the period, particularly on the Welsh side, should read sections of Thomas Jones, (ed.) *Brut y Tywysogyon or the Chronicle of the Princes: Peniarth MS 20 Version,* Cardiff, 1952, which is a translation of one version of the principal Welsh chronicle.

# Index

## The Places

# The Princes and their Allies

*Note:* In 13th-century Anglo-Welsh warfare, men changed sides often. Many of those listed below as allies of Llywelyn, in 1282, had earlier been among his enemies.

**83**

# Their Adversaries

# Others

# Subscribers
## Presentation Copies

1 The National Library of Wales
2 The Honourable Society of Cymmrodorion
3 Wadham College, Oxford
4 Sir Idris Ll Foster
5 Professor Rees Davies

6 David & Charlotte Stephenson
7 Clive & Carolyn Birch
8 Shropshire County
11 Library
12 Michael Llywelyn Price
13 S. Wegg-Prosser
14 Llanfairfechan Junior School
15 C.J. Holyoake
16 History Faculty Library, Oxford
17 O. Rocyn Jones
18 J. Wyn Evans
19 Dewi Jones
20 Irene H. Leet
21 Patrick Sims-Williams
22 Pauline Phillips
23 J.F. Morris
24 D.W. Smith
25 Miss F.K. Oakley
26 W.V. Shorto
27 C.L.J. Humphreys
28 John Hampson
29 Geoffrey Post
30 J.G.T. Sheringham
31 T. Ross Williams
32 Llanddeusant County Primary School
33 National Library of Wales
34 Robert J. Tomkins
35 Cranbrook School
36 Peter Chard
37 Simon C.J.F. Isbister
38 Mrs Nora M. Holliday-Rhodes

39 Victoria & Albert Museum
40 Donald F. Maclean
41 T.G.G. Herbert Ysw MRCUS
42 John Vivian Hughes
43 W.H. Adams
44 I.W. Prothero
45 John Howard Davies
46 Honourable Society of Cymmrodorion
47 J.M. Lewis
48 Gwynedd Library
56 Service
57 Brecon High School
58 
59 Gwent County Library
64 
65 Charles Evans FSA FSG
66 G.K. Dickson
67 Richard Morgan
68 Timothy Morgan
69 Richard H. Lewis
70 R. Cerdin Griffiths
71 Sydney Jones Library
72 Antony Beck
73 
74 Miss M.C. Williams
75 Afan AB Alun
76 R.R. Davies
77 Gwladys Hughes
78 Leslie & Marjorie Brooke
79 M.O. Wynne
80 A.D. Carr
81 Dr R.A. Griffiths

82 R.F. Stacey
83 Nesta Lloyd
84 
85 Dr Marshall Wilson
86 C.S.L. Davies
87 Glanmor Williams
88 Huw Pryce
89 Terence Harvey
90 Kenneth Ranforth Emmett
91 Michael Jackson
92 Jonathan Gross
93 R.G. Gruffydd
94 John David Rolant Thomas
95 T.R. Davies
96 Mr & Mrs Andrew Phillips
97 The Librarian, University College, 
98 Cardiff
99 Dafydd Jenkins
100 Morfydd E. Owen
101 Clwyd Library Service
102 Rhidian Griffiths
103 Major E.H.C. Davies
104 Acquisitions Librarian, University College of Wales
105 Rhondda Educational Centre
106 Newport Museum & Art Gallery
107 Mrs June Gruffydd
108 Avi Levine
109 Dr Michael Richter
110 Gareth Rhys Jones

212 D.H. Jones
213 T. Flynn
214 J.R. Brown
215 Mrs L.O. Larcombe
216 } Richard Glynne Jones
217
218 Maurice Richards
219 Dewi John Ward
220 K. Hubbard
221 Mrs A. Petty
222 D. Griffiths
223 John Bensusan-Butt
224 G.C. Coggins
225 } T.M. Charles-Edwards
226
227 } Lloyd Lloyd
228

229 Roger Phillips
230 Ifan Lloyd
231 Rhys Sutherland Thomas
232 Mark Iestyn Griffith
233 H.E. Francis QC
234 Mrs Mwynn Griffiths
235 Donald Moore
236 Sir Ernest Jones-Parry
237 B.G. Jones
238 Rev Charles Eurwyn Jones
239 Meurig Owen
240 W.L. Williams
241 David Lewellyn
242 A.M.C. Weale

243 Richard & Verona Morgan
244 Mr & Mrs W.D. White
245 Mrs L.D. Dicks
246 J. Philip Davies
247 } H.A. Prescott
248
249 Sir Idris Ll Foster
250 Bruce & Isabel Lorimer
251 Richard Butler
252 Tudor M. Hoell
253 Miss Susan E. Roberts
254 D.T.L. Clive Lewis
256 John Geeves
*Remaining names unlisted*